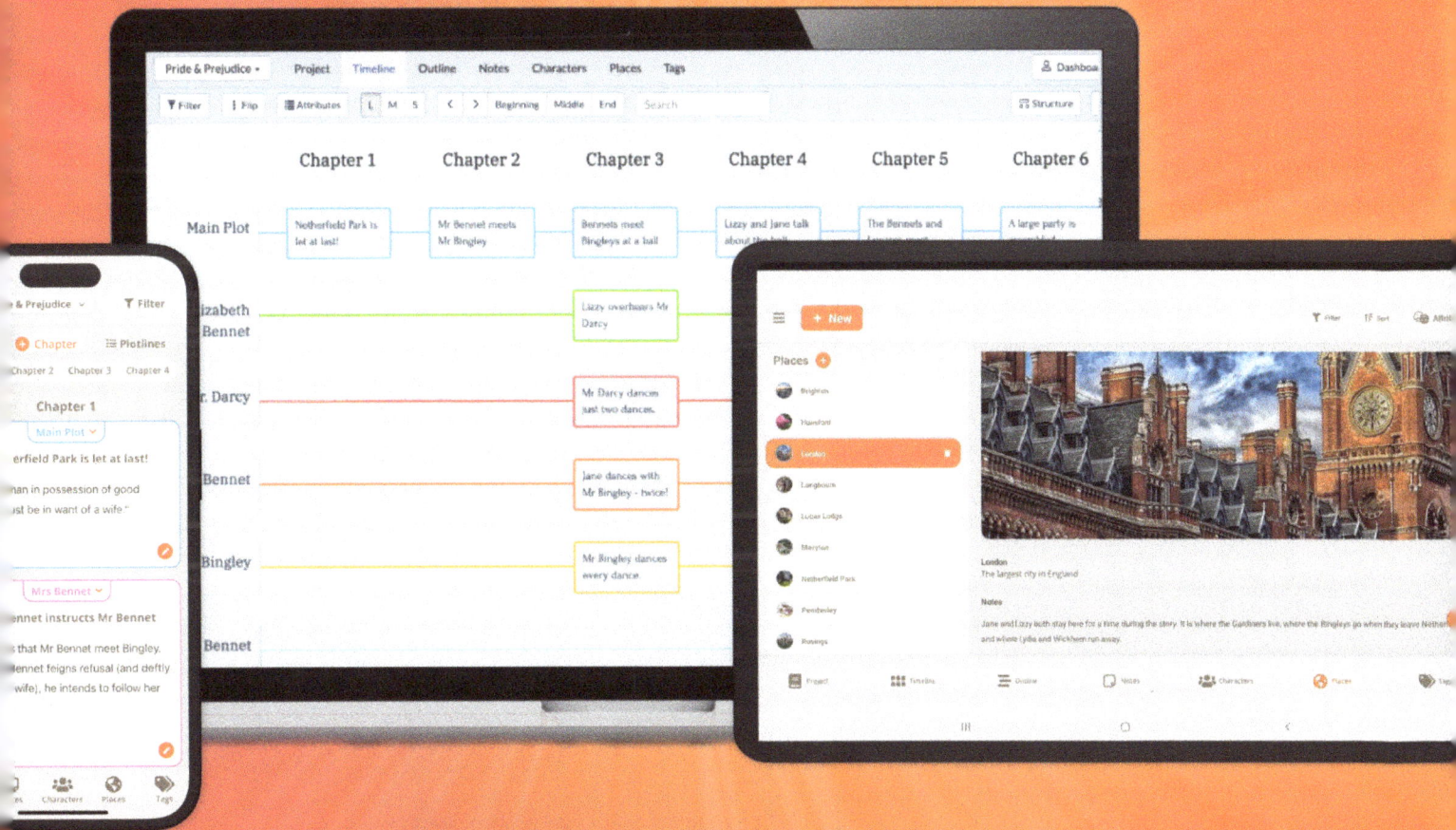

"I joined while having a crisis with Amazon KDP... The Alliance is a beacon of light. I recommend that all indie authors join...

**Susan Marshall**

"The Alliance is about standing together.

**Joanna Penn**

"It's the good stuff, all on one place.

**Richard Wright**

"ALLi has helped me in myriad ways: discounts on services, vetting providers, charting a course to sales success. But more than anything it's a community of friendly, knowledgeable, helpful people."

**Beth Duke**

See hundreds more testimonials at:
**AllianceIndependentAuthors.org/testimonials**

# IAM

## THE FUTURE OF PUBLISHING

# INDIE AUTHOR MAGAZINE

## HELLO AND WELCOME!

I'm Indie Annie, and I'm thrilled you're reading this gorgeous full-color version of IAM. Did you know that you can also access all the information, education, and inspiration in our app? It's available on both the iOS App Store and Google Play. And for those that prefer to listen to me read articles, you can pop over to Spotify or our website.
Happy Reading! X

IndieAuthorMagazine.com

# Authorpreneurs in Action

"I love Lulu! They've been a fantastic distributor of my paperbacks and an excellent partner as I dive into direct sales. They integrate so smoothly with my personal Shopify store, and their customer support has been top notch."

*Katie Cross, katiecrossbooks.com*

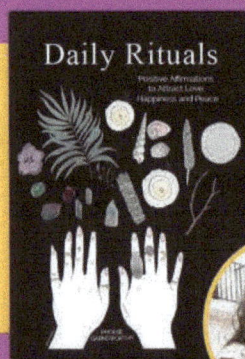

"Having my own store has given me the freedom to look at my creativity as a profitable business and lifelong career."

*Phoebe Garnsworthy, phoebegarnsworthy.com*

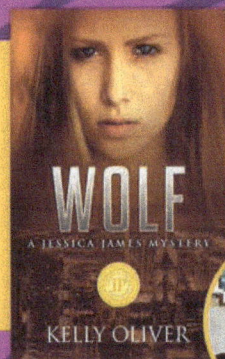

"Lulu has a super handy integration with Shopify. Lulu makes it so easy to sell paperbacks directly to readers."

*Kelly Oliver, kellyoliverbooks.com*

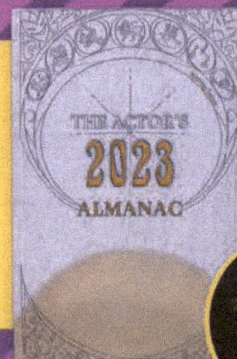

"My experience with Lulu Direct has been more convenient and simple than I anticipated or thought possible. I simply publish, take a step back and allow the well-oiled machine to run itself. Most grateful!"

*Molly McGivern, theactorsalmanac.com*

# INDIE
## AUTHOR MAGAZINE

### EDITORIAL

**Publisher** | Chelle Honiker

**Editor in Chief** | Nicole Schroeder

**Creative Director** | Alice Briggs

### ADVERTISING & MARKETING

**Inquiries**
Ads@AtheniaCreative.com

**Information**
https://IndieAuthorMagazine.com/
advertising/

### CONTRIBUTORS

Angela Archer, Elaine Bateman, Patricia Carr, Bradley Charbonneau, Honorée Corder, Jackie Dana, Heather Clement Davis, Jamie Davis, Laurel Decher, Fatima Fayez, Gill Fernley, Greg Fishbone, Jen B. Green, Jac Harmon, Marion Hermannsen, Steve Higgs, Chrishaun Keller-Hanna, Kasia Lasinska, Monica Leonelle, Jenn Lessmann, Megan Linski-Fox, Craig Martelle, Angie Martin, Merri Maywether, Kevin McLaughlin, Lasairiona McMaster, Jenn Mitchell, Tanya Nellestein, Russell Nohelty, Susan Odev, Eryka Parker, Tiffany Robinson, Clare Sager, Joe Solari, Becca Syme, David Viergutz

### SUBSCRIPTIONS
https://indieauthormagazine.com/subscribe/

### HOW TO READ
https://indieauthormagazine.com/how-to-read/

## WHEN WRITING MEANS BUSINESS
IndieAuthorMagazine.com

Athenia Creative | 6820 Apus Dr., Sparks, NV, 89436 USA | 775.298.1925

ISSN 2768-7880 (online)–ISSN 2768-7872 (print)

# From the
# EDITOR IN CHIEF

Think back to when you started your author career. When did you start to consider your brand, and how did you decide what it would be?

For me, the idea of settling on one selling point for my stories has always sounded nearly impossible. Even as I prepared to release my first book, I knew I would want to experiment with a variety of genres and writing styles in the future. Yet when I was building the foundation of my business and learning the ropes of social media marketing, newsletters, and managing my street team, doing all of that for a second pen name down the road sounded overwhelming.

This month's featured author, Dale Mayer, follows a different approach. She writes in a variety of genres, from Military Romance to New Adult vampire fiction. When she finds the topics in her Thriller Suspense stories getting too heavy, she gives herself a mental break with lighthearted Cozy Mystery romps. But Mayer doesn't feel the need to separate these stories across different pen names. Every story she publishes is under her own name, and her brand embraces the fact that her genre is always changing.

I've long admired the authors who are able to manage multiple pen names and brands, sometimes niching down even within specific subgenres so they can target exactly the readers who will be most interested in a particular series. In some genres, it's almost required—ask the Romance author who likes to dabble in both Sweet stories and those that are spicier.

But Mayer's approach deserves our applause too.

From its inception, *IAM* articles have reinforced that there is no right way to be an indie author. As you'll read in this month's cover feature, Mayer's story, with all its successes, is proof. Whether your brand is a narrow, genre-specific funnel meant to draw in only the most ardent fans or an all-encompassing portrait of your author career for your readers to explore, there's an audience for the stories you want to write and a way to connect with them.

Storytelling is an endlessly creative pursuit; in this issue and every other issue, we hope our articles prove that your business can be too.

Nicole Schroeder
Editor in Chief
*Indie Author Magazine*

Nicole Schroeder is a storyteller at heart. As the editor in chief of Indie Author Magazine, she brings nearly a decade of journalism and editorial experience to the publication, delighting in any opportunity to tell true stories and help others do the same. She holds a bachelor's degree from the Missouri School of Journalism and minors in English and Spanish. Her previous work includes editorial roles at local publications, and she's helped edit and produce numerous fiction and nonfiction books, including a Holocaust survivor's memoir, alongside independent publishers. Her own creative writing has been published in national literary magazines. When she's not at her writing desk, Nicole is usually in the saddle, cuddling her guinea pigs, or spending time with family. She loves any excuse to talk about Marvel movies and considers National Novel Writing Month its own holiday.

PLANNING TRAVEL TO A CONFERENCE?

Use miles.

Explore ways to make the most of your award miles.

Writelink.to/unitedair

# STORYTELLER
## OPERATING SYSTEM

### NOTION FOR AUTHORS

### LEARN:

The PARA Method for Writers
Building Your Story Bible
Setting up Books and Series
Task Management for Writing
Task Management for Editing, ARCs, and Betas
Collaborating in Notion
Incorporating other Apps into Notion
Automating Workflows
And More!

SIGN UP: INDIEAUTHORTRAINING.COM

# MARTELLE'S MOTIVATION

# The Time Is Now

I submit that there has never been a better time to be a writer. We have to highlight the change in the publishing landscape and the advances in opportunity between 2009 and 2017—most notably the windfalls that came with public acceptance of e-books and the viability of self-publishing thanks to Amazon.

Traditional publishers had their methodologies for selecting authors to reward with contracts and advance royalties. Many good authors were pushed aside because their stories didn't fit with what a publisher was selling. That makes sense. Who wants a product they don't think they can sell? But that barrier to entry has been removed. Some may contend that bad books predominate on Amazon, as there is no gatekeeper to keep them out.

Is that what the twelve publishers are saying who rejected *Harry Potter and the Philosopher's Stone*?

I suggest that the greatest arbiter of a good book is the reader. Bad books will fall by the wayside. Good books will see the light of day, but only if the readers consider them good. The challenge is how to find those readers, and self-published authors are exploring innovative ways to contact and expand their readership.

Who am I to make these claims? I run a group with over 75,000 self-published authors. We share best business practices. We share successes. We don't promote to one another; our fellow authors are not our target audience. Readers are. They are varied and sometimes elusive, but they're out there. I wouldn't have been able to sell a

million books without the knowledge I've learned in that group. And I'm still learning something new every day. This business isn't static. It's constantly evolving.

What we have now are ways for authors to improve: to get feedback, rewrite, and try again. We have extensive market experience to advertise to a narrower audience, specifically those who could like our books. You'll find that some of us have reader numbers that any traditional publisher would envy. Self-published authors—"indies," as we call ourselves—are shoulder to shoulder as we learn how to sell to the reading public.

The self-publication model is far different and more appealing to today's audience. Our e-books aren't priced to make physical books more attractive. Self-published authors can price an e-book at $5, and pocket $3.75 from the sale.

Marketing is more challenging now than it was just two years ago, but groups like 20BooksTo50k® and Successful Indie Author break down the walls to understanding. It is easier now than ever before to learn what you need to know when you need to know it. Being an author is a lonely business, but we don't have to be alone. It is not a zero-sum game. One reader can read more books than we can write, and they will read the books they like, no matter who published them.

Most of the full-time authors I know, including me, are making a full-time living, many reaching seven figures a year. There's never been a better time.

A rising tide lifts all boats. ∎

Craig Martelle

## Craig Martelle

High school Valedictorian enlists in the Marine Corps under a guaranteed tank contract. An inauspicious start that was quickly superseded by excelling in language study. Contract waived, a year at the Defense Language Institute to learn Russian and off to keep my ears on the big red machine during the Soviet years. Earned a four-year degree in two years by majoring in Russian Language. My general staff. career included choice side gigs – UAE, Bahrain, Korea, Russia, and Ukraine.

Major Martelle. I retired from the Marines after a couple years at the embassy in Moscow working arms control issues.

Department of Homeland Security then law school next. I was working for a high-end consulting firm performing business diagnostics, business law, and leadership coaching. For the money they paid me, I was good with that. Just until I wasn't. Then I started writing.

# The Power of Past Titles

The term "backlist" is one self-publishing authors adopted from traditional publishers, though it's less relevant in the days of digital publishing than it was when only the frontlist—the newest books—got the most attention from readers. Today, we can promote any book, any time, and though your latest book is often your highest-earning book for a period, most authors find it's their backlist that brings in the cash consistently. So what should you be doing to capitalize on your backlist? How do you maximize the benefits of every title you publish? What tactics work best?

The Alliance of Independent Authors's (ALLi's) detailed blog post on this topic, "Boost Your Backlist: How to Make the Most of Every Title," includes practical tips from successful indie authors on how they keep their own backlists up to date. Meanwhile, for whatever stage you're at, here are some extra suggestions.

## BEGINNER AUTHORS:
## THINK LONG-TERM

From your earliest days as an author, think ahead for the long run and not just about your first book—even though, of course, it will always be special to you. When choosing an imprint or publishing name, pick something generic that will suit all your future books, not something near-identical to your first title. When choosing a URL for your website, choose your own author name and not the book title. If you have a series planned, put the second book title on preorder as quickly as you can so that you get a series page on most big retail platforms. Make sure you have a list of current and forthcoming books in the back matter so you can already list the next book you'll be publishing.

Some new authors focus just on a paperback, when an e-book is not just an important extra format but, especially for fiction, likely to outsell the paperback. For a successful long-term business, ALLi recommends going as wide as possible, both in terms of platforms and formats. It can also be useful to create the time and connections needed to keep an eye on the publishing industry and your section of it so you can monitor how it changes over time. Even a twice-yearly investigation of the industry and your genre for half an hour on a big platform like Amazon will quickly show you if there are new cover trends developing or a new style of blurb being written. This will enable you to better manage your own backlist as it develops.

## EMERGING AUTHORS:
## GO BACK TO BASICS

It is tempting to feel you've done all the basics for your back catalog: the covers, blurbs, keywords, and categories. But trends come and go, and it's important to keep an eye on your existing titles and the market. If a new keyword arises, are you making the most of it? If a category is dropped or created, have you updated your preferences? Your cover may start to look tired, or blurbs may change in style. Over a longer period, even interior layout styles change. It's worth setting aside time every year to review these elements and consider whether any of them need refreshing. At the very least, your front and back matter may well need a refresh as your bio changes, as you publish new books, or as you add a reader magnet and a mailing list to your marketing toolkit. You may wish to change up your calls-to-action as your marketing needs change. Every book is new to a new reader … unless it's looking tired and unloved.

While reviewing these elements, you can also consider whether you now have the funds or time to add new formats, such as translations or audiobooks, that perhaps were outside of your budget until now. ALLi's blog has posts on both.

For audiobooks, visit: https://selfpublishingadvice.org/the-ultimate-guide-to-audiobooks-for-authors

For translations, visit: https://selfpublishingadvice.org/the-ultimate-guide-to-book-translations-for-indie-authors

## EXPERIENCED AUTHORS: EXPLORE FURTHER

All experienced authors can benefit from exploring licensing rights. Your books are not just books; they are creative intellectual property (IP), and as such, they have the potential to be used in myriad ways, from films and TV to games and apps. Explore ALLi's book *How Authors Sell Publishing Rights* to look into the opportunities available to you, available at https://selfpublishingadvice.org/bookshop.

Once an author dies, their works are still in copyright for seventy years, yet according to ALLi's 2023 Independent Author Income Survey, only 25 percent of full-time authors had made a will covering their literary estate and how to manage it. ALLi recommends authors prioritize writing such a will or adding to one they already have. ALLi members

have access to two free books: one on how to set up your literary estate and the other a handbook for an author's heirs to guide them through how to best manage a literary estate. After all, seventy years of sales for your complete creative catalog are not to be sniffed at.

Finally, what is the most likely marketing tool you will use to showcase our backlist? Your mailing list, of course—and that also needs looking after and updating, just like your backlist. Is your autoresponder sequence up to date? Does your newsletter signature include all your book covers? Are you regularly cleaning your subscriber list? Because your mailing list is so important for all aspects of your business, including your backlist, ALLi has a three-part mailing list series, titled "The Ultimate Guide to Email Marketing for Authors," available on its blog at https://selfpublishingadvice.org:

Part 1: Mailing List Strategy
Part 2: Growing Your Reader Email List(s)
Part 3: Maintaining your Reader Email List

Additionally, in its *Self-Publishing Advice & Inspirations* podcast, ALLi presented an episode on the topic for beginners. Find the podcast episode at: https://selfpublishingadvice.org/building-a-mailing-list.

Rather than a tedious administrative task, see the curation and care of your backlist as a golden opportunity to make its contents shine anew in the eyes of your readers. ∎

Melissa Addey, ALLi Campaigns Manager

### Melissa Addey, ALLi's Campaign Manager

The Alliance of Independent Authors (ALLi) is a global membership association for self-publishing authors. A non-profit, our mission is ethics and excellence in self-publishing. Everyone on our team is a working indie author and we offer advice and advocacy for self-publishing authors within the literary, publishing and creative industries around the world. www.allianceindependentauthors.org

# Dear Indie Annie,

**Despite my best marketing efforts, my backlist just isn't selling. How do I decide whether to go back to the drawing board and refocus the series or cut my losses and unpublish it?**

**At a Crossroads**

## Dear Crossroads,

I feel your frustration, love. When a backlist underperforms, it's like owning a vintage auto that sputters more than it purrs. Do you tune it up or trade it in for a new model? Let's hash out indie author strategies.

First, diagnose if it's truly a lemon or just needs maintenance. Some classics stay road-worthy for decades with care. Consider Jane Austen's *Emma* or Agatha Christie's Poirot Mysteries—loyal fans span generations. Maybe your baby just needs a tune-up. Don't junk durable stories without considering an overhaul.

But if foundational features feel irreparable, could you envision radical customization? Trick out characters, settings, or other elements to reinvent the vehicle. Rework it into something unrecognizable, like custom car shops turning beaters into hot rods.

I will admit to a tiny little guilty pleasure here, dear Crossroads: I love watching episodes of *American Chopper*. Messrs. Paul Teutul Sr. and Jr. could take this creaky chassis out for a ride anytime. But I digress …

Your vintage collection may seem a tad shaky, but are they truly ready for the scrapyard just yet? A complete overhaul may be radical if all they need is some TLC.

The beauty of self-publishing is total creative control. Although traditional contracts limit remixing published works, indies can retool at will. Rescitate stale stories through extensive edits, new covers, and

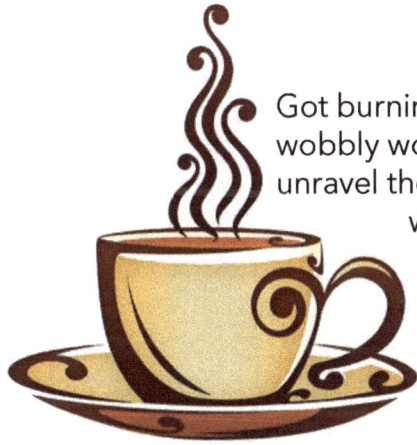

Got burning questions about the wibbly-wobbly world of indie authoring? Eager to unravel the mysteries of publishing, writing woes, or anything in between? Give your quizzical quills a whirl and shoot your musings over to indieannie@indieauthormagazine.com. Your inky quandaries are my cup of tea!

bonus materials like author forewords. Even switch up genres and target audiences. The flexibility to overhaul your catalog keeps classics roadworthy.

Are foundational elements sound but sales sluggish? I mentioned Austen and Christie earlier. Google or check out Pinterest to see the range of covers they have worn over the decades, each one bringing the same classic stories to a whole new generation. Or think of the many film and TV adaptations of their works. Why not try the same strategy with your story, refreshing the covers, trying different formats, or expanding into new territories with transmedia?

You can always refresh and retarget promotion. Analyze reviews to highlight untapped hooks for new readers. Revamp book blurbs and pitches. Advertise in niche communities aligned with adjustments to your work. Update keywords for discovery. Self-publishing grants the artistic freedom to reposition titles for renewed momentum.

Of course, sometimes older models grow too dated. If you decide these old bangers are not even fit for a stock car derby, scrap what no longer thrills you. Trust your gut, and shift gears to draft fresh adventures fine-tuned for who you are today.

Every author spins out or stalls sometimes. View past mishaps not as defeat but as practice in resilience. Ditch draining projects and focus on smoothing your ride. And remember, stories that sputtered before may find new life later when retooled with hard-won skills. The classics endure!

Keep cruising with spirit! Your best adventures lie ahead. Meanwhile, I'm going to check out some reruns of *American Chopper* with a steaming hot cup of tea.

Happy writing,
Indie Annie
X

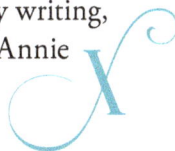

# 10 TIPS FOR
## CRAFTING THE PERFECT BLURB

When it comes to the back cover blurb, many authors think they have to summarize their entire ninety-thousand-word novel in just a few lines. But a successful blurb is not meant to be a summary of your novel. It's a sales pitch to nudge people into buying it. It's time to shift how you think of your book's description from an exercise in crushing your plot into less than two hundred fifty words to a chance to highlight the moments that are going to make people read, click, and buy.

Here are our ten best tips to producing a blurb that entices and converts.

---

### 1 KNOW YOUR AUDIENCE

When writing a blurb, your goal should be to include what will appeal to your readers and make them want to pick up your book. In order to do that, you have to know your audience. Who do you write for? What do they look for in your genre? Examine your story's themes and tropes and the elements that your audience will connect with the most, so you can be sure to add those to your blurb.

---

### 2 LOOK AT THE TOP SELLING BOOKS IN YOUR GENRE

"After the title and the book cover, your description is the most important book marketing material," according to Scribe Media. The best-selling books in your genre have that title for a reason, so where better to look for examples of what works?

As you read through each, note details like which tense they use, whether they are written from the character's point of view, the plot points they highlight, and how they entice you to read more. Then, try to do the same with your novel and create something that reads as though it fits in with those top selling books.

## 3 DON'T OVERTHINK IT

When it's time to write, set aside a block of time to focus entirely on your blurb, and turn off your inner editor. Approach this brainstorming session the same way you did writing sprints for your book's first draft.

If you're stuck, start by picking out as many highlights from your book as you can that might appeal to readers, as well as any relevant story details readers should know at the start of the first chapter, such as character names or world-building elements.

**Pro Tip:** Think of your blurb like a movie trailer—the best ones draw audiences into the story by emphasizing the stakes and leaving readers with more questions than answers.

---

## 4 USE A FORMULA IF IT HELPS

If you're struggling, following a formula for your blurb can make it easier. Once you have the general bones, you can tweak it until you're happy with it and add more emotion and tropes to make it your own.

James Scott Bell offers a simple formula in his Knockout Novel software:

- First Sentence: Your character's name, vocation, and initial situation
- Second Sentence: "When" plus the first doorway of no return
- Third Sentence: "Now" plus death overhanging

Note: Death overhanging doesn't necessarily mean actual death. It could be emotional or psychological death.

Just those three sentences can get you away from the blank page and give you something you can edit, which is often half the battle. If you add the plot of *Star Wars: Episode IV—A New Hope* to that formula, here's what you get:

Luke Skywalker, a farm boy, is stuck on the desert world of Tatooine, though he longs for adventure in space.

When he uncovers a desperate message for help from Princess Leia Organa, his aunt and uncle are killed by Imperial troops in search of the droid containing the message, and he finds himself in danger.

Now, he's aboard the Millenium Falcon with a space pirate, a giant Wookie, and the princess, with the might of the Galactic Empire in pursuit. Can the small band of rebels destroy the deadly Death Star space station before it destroys them and ends the rebellion for good?

**Pro Tip:** A quick Google will bring you a variety of blurb formulae. Experiment with a few of them until you find one you prefer.

## 5 CONSIDER EMOTION, CONFLICT, AND STAKES

Bryan Cohen, the CEO of Best Page Forward, says his best advice for blurb writing is focusing on the emotional journey your character takes in your novel. "Too many authors focus on the plot, but plots are a dime a dozen," he says. "If you concentrate on how a character reacts to the plot throughout your blurb, then you have a better chance of getting your reader to react as well. Making an emotional connection at this stage of the game is key to getting readers to click the buy button."

Consider the emotional moments of your novel, where your protagonist faces mounting stakes or reaches a turning point and is forced to shift their perspective. If there's a plot twist you're expecting will make your readers gasp, hint at it when you write your blurb.

## 6 LEAVE THEM HANGING

When writing a blurb, you're almost writing a new, very short story to entice readers and leave them wanting more. And of course, they can only get more by buying your book.

"Blurbs are hard to write, and every single word must count," says Robert J. Ryan, author of *Book Blurbs Unleashed*. "But the ending is critical. Finish on a cliffhanger, with a story twist to give it even more punch, and leave the reader desperate to know what happens next. Your conversion rate will climb."

Not only should you not tell people the whole story, but you should also deliberately leave questions unanswered and possibly even end with a full-on cliffhanger.

## 7 KEYWORD IT

Amazon is a big online bookstore, but it's also a massive search engine. As you're tweaking your book's description, consider the terms your readers search for, and work those words and phrases into your blurb. Mentioning tropes and themes in your blurb makes it even more enticing and easier to find among the millions of other books online.

## 8 GET FEEDBACK

Once you're ready, share your blurb with trusted writer friends—and maybe even some of your readers—and ask for their thoughts. Are there details that confuse them? Did they reach the end and need to know more?

You get to make the final decision on what your blurb looks like, but if several people make similar comments, it's worth listening to them.

## 9   POLISH IT UP

Kindlepreneur offers a free book description generator for Amazon, Barnes & Noble, and Kobo that allows authors to generate the HTML code needed to format their blurb for different platforms.

However, the tool now includes an AI element, connecting to ChatGPT, that breaks down the description into elements like "hook," "setting," "main character," and "suspenseful sentence" and suggests revisions to make it more attention-grabbing.

This part of the tool is optional but can generate ideas you can take or leave. It's your blurb, after all. Paste any parts of the AI blurb that you want to use into the generator, edit them as necessary, then click "Go Back to Formatting," and you'll be able to regenerate your code.

---

## 10   REFINE, EDIT, AND TEST

Don't put pressure on yourself to come up with the perfect blurb immediately. You might write something good enough for now and then keep tweaking it until you find you're making more sales. You can always edit your description down the road, even after the book has been published, so if you're not sold, try cycling out several descriptions until you find one that works. Just be sure not to change anything else at the same time. If you also change your cover, for example, you'll have no idea which change made the difference in sales. ∎

Gill Fernley

### Gill Fernley

Gill Fernley writes fiction in several genres under different pen names, but what all of them have in common is humor and romance, because she can't resist a happy ending or a good laugh. She's also a freelance content writer and has been running her own business since 2013. Before that, she was a technical author and documentation manager for an engineering company and can describe to you more than you'd ever wish to know about airflow and filtration in downflow booths. Still awake? Wow, that's a first! Anyway, that experience taught her how to explain complex things in straightforward language and she hopes it will come in handy for writing articles for IAM. Outside of writing, she's a cake decorator, expert shoe hoarder, and is fluent in English, dry humor and procrastibaking.

# Unlocking the Storyteller

## HOW DALE MAYER SHUTS DOWN INTRUSIVE THOUGHTS AND RELEASES THE WORDS

A hostage situation wouldn't be out of place in any of Dale Mayer's Military Romance series. It might not even be completely unexpected in one of her Thriller Suspense series, or in a novel from her Paranormal catalog. So when she talks about some of the unusual steps she takes to release her creative mind, somehow, they all make sense. After all, any successful rescue mission is going to require a detailed plan of attack and maybe a good distraction.

USA TODAY bestselling author Dale Mayer promises "a great read each and every time," whether that read follows the adventures of a team of military veterans and their highly trained war dogs or an amateur sleuth in small-town Canada. Best known for her Psychic Visions series, Dale "honors the stories that come to her," she says, writing so many books across multiple genres that her website now includes three separate flowcharts to help readers find their way. There are over two hundred fifty books listed, not including box sets or the nineteen books she has on preorder.

### AWARENESS

Dale began her writing career writing five thousand words of fiction a day while doing technical writing to pay the bills, but somehow, the breakneck speed she's maintained from the start hasn't slowed. In the fall of 2000, Dale won fourth place in a writing contest that came with the opportunity to

work with an agent. She was excited at first, but she ultimately decided to self-publish after the agent encouraged her to cut a character she loved from her debut. She released the first three books in her Psychic Visions series in rapid succession.

Then she switched, temporarily, to the Young Adult genre. Dale's teenage daughter was craving vampire fiction at the time and couldn't find what she wanted on the shelves. Her obliging mother composed a ten-book series, which will soon be re-released for a New Adult audience with aged-up characters. Although her daughter outgrew vampires somewhere around book seven, she remains involved in Dale's business, handling some of the marketing and social media to give her mother more time to focus on the creative side.

different. Everybody was doing what worked for them," she says. Based on this knowledge, she decided the best way forward was to "stop looking outside. Just write what you want to write. Promote it as much as you can, and if it doesn't sell, either move on or keep writing because it brings you joy."

She started writing Military Romance around 2016, enjoying the fast-paced action that provided a break from her more complicated Mysteries. Now she has one hundred fifty of them published alongside her Thrillers and a newer series of Cozy Mysteries. She says they're fun and easy to write and grins talking about some of the ideas she has for new stories. "What you want to do is unlock your storyteller. I would consider myself a storyteller versus a writer," she says.

## ASSESSMENT

In 2015, after she noticed a drop in sales, Dale started researching successful authors. She interviewed several of her friends to see what they were doing. What she found surprised her. "Everybody was doing something

## ACTION

Of course, how authors get the words on the page is just as important as the craft that goes into their stories. For Dale, the answer has always been quickly—even if the actual method has varied over time.

A few years ago, Dale gave an interview describing how she had written nine thousand words before breakfast. Although she was happy with her writing speed, regularly typing twelve thousand to thirteen thousand words per day, Dale's knuckles eventually started to complain. It took three tries for her to switch to dictating, but by 2016, she made it stick. Now she dictates ten thousand words in an hour, finishing one-hundred-thousand-word Thrillers in two weeks. Dale does most of her dictation in the morning, but she keeps an 8 a.m. to 4 p.m. work schedule. After she gets her words in, she switches to the business side: advertising, direct sales, and community building. The books are page-turners, no matter which genre, and her readers are always asking for more.

Dale's storyteller, the creative side of her mind, comes out when she manages to distract the rest of her brain. "There's all those other things—intrusive thoughts that come in all the time to everybody's brain—and so trying to stay focused for me means shutting that part off, and the way to shut that off for me means [I need to] give it a task. So you're occupying it with something else. I am giving it something to do. And while it's doing that, this half is free," she says.

For a while, it was enough for Dale to go for a walk, dictating her story as she moved down a path or circled her property. But the weather doesn't always permit an unfocused ramble, and occasionally she'd get too wrapped up in the story to pay attention to where she was going. For her own safety, she needed an alternative.

Though many authors listen to music while they write, that technique doesn't work as well when you're dictating a story. So Dale started watching movies with the sound off. After trying a few different films, she found that some—Disney's *Moana* in particular—worked better for her than others. She had to know the movie well enough not to get sucked into the plot. It had to be predictable enough to let her creative mind wander but challenging enough to engage her analytical side.

Eventually, however, she still needed more. Dale switched to playing solitaire on her phone, and when that became too easy, she upgraded to spider solitaire, then jigsaw puzzles. When the puzzles stop engaging her executive functioning, she moves up to more difficult ones, thousands of pieces spread out in front of her while she dictates.

After two weeks of dictation, the recordings of her finished draft, complete with the occasional author note, doorbell, or curse of frustration when she forgets a character's name, go on to a transcriptionist. Dale says she tried voice-to-text apps like Dragon for transcribing her work, but the AI had trouble with her Canadian accent and made too many mistakes in the manuscripts. She works with two transcribers who type out her words faithfully and send the file back to her. Meanwhile, she's already recording the next book.

The manuscript Dale receives from her transcribers is still almost four months from being ready for publication, though she says she could streamline that process to one month if needed. But she probably won't ever need to. Although Dale publishes an average of two books per month, she's already completed enough books to get her most of the way through the next year. Remember all those preorders? Those books are finished and ready for readers before they go up on her website.

"I decided a few years back I was tired of living on the cliff edge of deadlines, and I really put my nose to the grindstone, and I just got a year in advance," she says. Dale took advantage of COVID lockdowns to concentrate on finishing as many books as she could, as quickly as possible. Now her preorders go up, as completed projects, a year ahead of their release. Most series are on a schedule, releasing at the same time each year, but she has some room to squeeze in new projects if they arise. She skips most of the usual social media pre-launch campaigns, like excerpts and cover reveals, except for what is needed for her newsletter.

Her system is pretty seamless, despite the number of steps involved. She's found ways to get help with "the tedious kind of jobs that I don't have time for," which leaves her free for creative work, she says. Once she gets the manuscript back from the transcribers, she prints it and edits it by hand. Then she sends it to someone who enters all the edits for her. The edited

manuscript goes to a developmental editor, who usually reads it and returns it in a day, mostly checking for consistency. Dale revises any of the continuity errors, again by hand, before sending it to a line editor. Then she revises again and sends it to proofreaders, beta readers, and another round of proofreaders. When she's happy with the manuscript, it goes to a formatter, who sends it back to her for one last check before it gets uploaded. She has two full-time employees, who usually do the final upload and manage her store.

## AFTERCARE

Dale's first books were Thrillers, and she has continued writing in dark genres, hoping "to bring some of those [real-life dark experiences] to light in the world out there," she says. But years of writing in darkness took its toll on her mental health. She started writing Cozy Mysteries, set in her own hometown, as an escape. The Lovely Lethal Gardens series provides her an opportunity to share her sense of humor while challenging herself to develop the clues. Dale says changing genres keeps her from burning out because it's "fun and always different." Many of her readers agree, following her author brand across genres. She says she sees crossover from Thrillers to Cozies, and from Cozies to Military Romance. Only the Paranormal readers seem to stay in their silo, but that may change when her YA vampire series gets reintroduced to a New Adult audience.

She titles her Cozy Mysteries alphabetically,

and after seeing the disappointment from Sue Grafton's readers when the author passed away without finishing *Z is for Zero* in her Mystery series, Dale prioritized completing hers. "You know, I don't have any health concerns or anything like that," she assures me. But "it's nice to know that you have twenty or thirty books in the wing. For a lot of authors, that's a lifetime." Having so many books prepared lets her consider other ways of spending her time, like taking a cruise with writer friends, volunteering with animal rescues and women's shelters, or advising new authors. She was able to take a few months off last year because of the backlog of preorders she'd set up.

As she looks to the future, Dale says she'd eventually like to shorten her work week, maybe take Fridays off for some of those activities. She's confident that she'll be able to maintain her business because of the people who help get her books out. She says having a good team to make the books the best they can be also helps her to "find a schedule that makes everybody happy."

This sense of the value of teamwork and lessons learned from experience permeates her books, whether it's the SEAL teams in her Military Romances or the animal friends in her Cozy Mysteries. But ultimately, Dale's brand is built on herself. Even her merchandise bears her monogram. So when asked how she would advise others trying to rescue their creative minds, Dale says, "There's a story inside you. It's your story. Make it yours. Don't be swayed by anybody else. Keep it yours, and trust that other people will enjoy that bit of you." ■

Jenn Lessmann

### Jenn Lessmann

Jenn Lessmann is the author of Unmagical: a Witchy Mystery and three stories on Kindle Vella. A former barista, stage manager, and high school English teacher with advanced degrees from impressive colleges, she continues to drink excessive amounts of caffeine, stay up later than is absolutely necessary, and read three or four books at a time. Jenn is currently studying witchcraft and the craft of writing, and giggling internally whenever they intersect. She writes snarky paranormal fantasy for new adults whenever her dog will allow it.

# Breathing New Life into Your Backlist

## A GUIDE TO COVER REVITALIZATION

The terms of independent publishing are ever-evolving as authors constantly seek ways to expand their readership. To secure shelf space among competitive titles in the marketplace, authors can benefit from exploring ways to rejuvenate their backlist catalog in order to boost sales.

Although we're cautioned against judging a book by its cover, readers often decide to explore a book's pages based on the allure of that first impression. This explains why one of the most impactful trends in reintroducing older titles is revitalizing book covers according to modern styles and trends. There are other reasons to refresh your backlist's covers as well; some authors are no longer pleased with their original covers and are ready for a new look and feel for their previously published books.

A cover revitalization strategy can help catch the eyes of potential readers, rekindle interest in your titles, and give your cover a fresh look that will help your readers identify your genre. However, the decision to invest in a cover overhaul can require consideration of several factors, including timing, cost, and whether it's better to choose a selective approach or a comprehensive overhaul.

### KEY CONSIDERATIONS

Each year, over one million book titles are independently published. While other aspects of marketing and metadata also impact your book's success, the cover is often the initial touchpoint for potential readers, helping draw their attention while conveying important information about the story and genre. To successfully navigate the cover redesign decision process, authors must ensure their time and monetary investments will yield the desired results.

Writer can draw the attention of loyal readers, as well as collectors on BookTok and Bookstagram, by introducing limited and special edition books of backlist titles with new covers. Dedicated readers may buy new versions of the books they already own when newly designed covers are released, especially when the variant covers belong to a flagship series.

The first step to deciding whether to rebrand a series with new covers, then, is to understand the reasons behind your desire to update your covers, as well as the advantages of the decision.

- **A modernized cover design can lead to increased visibility and appeal.** A fresh, eye-catching cover can attract new readers who may have previously overlooked your book. According to the marketing principle known as "the rule of seven," it takes an average of seven impressions before a reader will take action and purchase your book. New covers may draw potential readers who previously overlooked your title back to the purchase page.

- **Emulating market trends can help with genre identification.** Each genre has specific design elements readers associate with and expect from its covers. These components change over time, so studying the market is important to staying abreast of modern design.

- **Book cover redesign can help reach new potential audiences.** Adapting to current design and genre trends can make a book more appealing to contemporary audiences. Redesigning your cover can attract new readers and connect you with untapped markets and demographics who weren't drawn by the original design.

While the advantages are enticing, it's equally important to navigate through the key considerations when contemplating a backlist cover redesign.

- **The opportunity may not always justify the cost.** A cover revamp can require a significant financial investment, so it's important to weigh the potential returns against the upfront expenses. Is this a true necessity at this time, or are there less expensive marketing techniques—such as discounting older titles, collaborating with book reviewers, or placing social media ads—that can yield similar results?

- **New market trends may interfere with brand consistency.** Introducing a new, enticing cover can seem exciting, but it should also help you maintain brand continuity for your existing readers. A drastic change in your backlist covers shouldn't confuse your current audience. Consider how to balance your existing and new designs in a way that will resonate with your current readers and appeal to new ones.

- **It can be difficult to manage reader expectations.** Your long-time readers may have grown attached to your original covers. Ensure that your changes are not so drastic that they confuse your readers. They may have certain expectations concerning a book's visual representation in terms of its consistency with the rest of the series and with other titles in its genre.

## TIMING IS EVERYTHING

So when is it the ideal time to take on a cover overhaul project? There's no right answer, but it's important to consider factors such as sales trajectory, reader feedback, and shifts in the dynamic of your genre. For series writers, it's a good idea to wait until the full series is well established before considering a book cover revamp. This helps with visual cohesion and recognition, cultivating emotional connection, and building reader anticipation.

## COST-EFFECTIVE STRATEGIES

Revitalizing covers doesn't always have to break the bank. There are many cost-effective strategies to explore.

- **DIY Design:** If you have a background in graphic design and have studied the market, you can opt to leverage design software and templates to take a hands-on approach to cover design. For your first few attempts, you may want to request feedback from a trusted expert, readers of your genre, or even an experienced librarian or bookseller.
- **Collaborative Approaches:** Partnering with a freelance designer for valuable insights can keep costs manageable. Some book review platforms, like NetGalley, poll their audiences for cover feedback and allow submissions of older titles for review. This grants access to a community of professional readers, librarians, booksellers, educators, and media members to offer feedback and expand your reach to a broader audience.

- **Testing the Waters:** Opting to pilot changes on a single title before committing to a full series overhaul is a cost-effective option that allows space for feedback from both new and existing audiences.

## SELECTIVE APPROACH OR COMPREHENSIVE OVERHAUL?

When contemplating a cover redesign, authors often grapple with the decision to redesign an entire series at once. This decision can impact the consistency of the series, brand identity, and reader expectations—not to mention the upfront expense for the author.

Taking a selective approach can allow authors to assess reader feedback before committing to a full series redesign. It can also be a more cost-effective approach for authors on a tight budget. On the other hand, it can be challenging to maintain a balance between consistency and innovation to avoid confusion among long-time readers. Also, the selection of books for redesign within a catalog or series must be strategic to maximize impact.

Doing a comprehensive overhaul, however, ensures visual cohesion throughout the entire series, enhancing brand recognition. It also provides a fresh, unified look that represents a committed effort to revitalize the author's body of work. Alternatively, taking on a full cover redesign overhaul

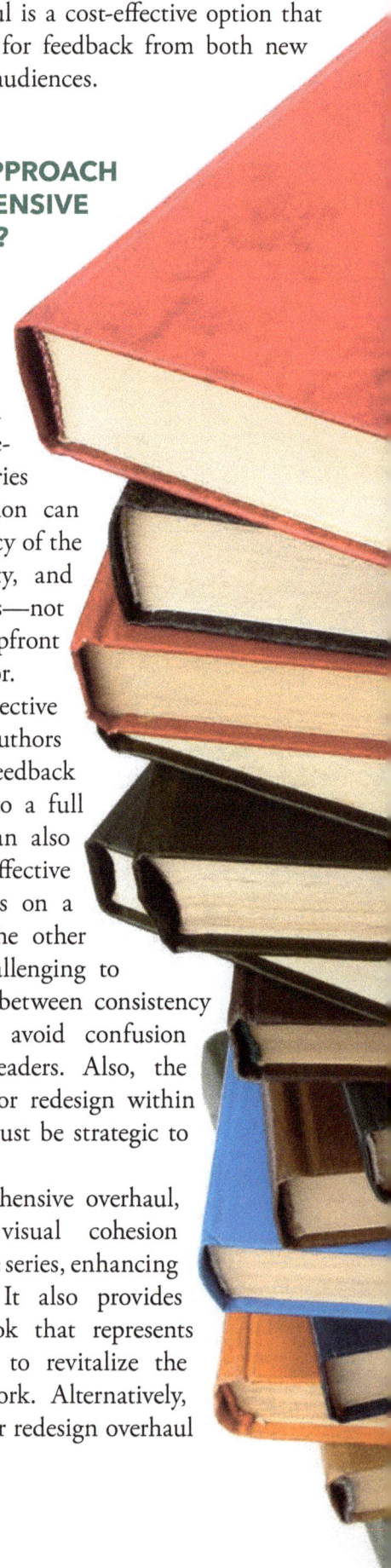

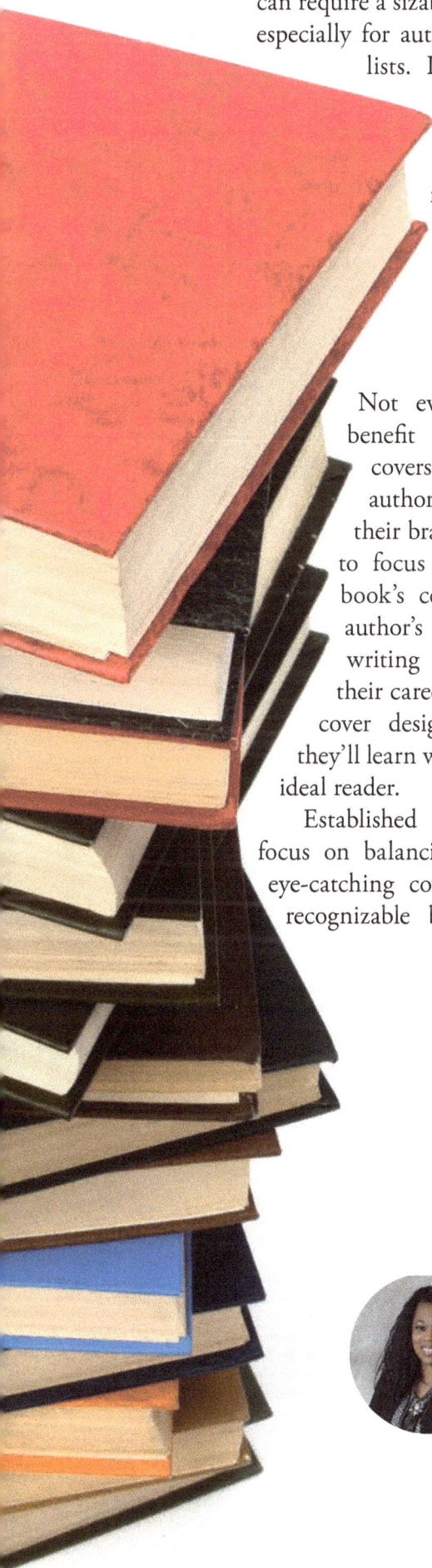

can require a sizable financial commitment, especially for authors with extensive back-lists. It's beneficial to conduct in-depth market research and careful planning to avoid overwhelming readers and committing to a fleeting trend.

## AUTHOR SKILL LEVEL

Not every author is likely to benefit from revitalizing their covers to the same degree. New authors who are still establishing their brand would likely do better to focus on covers that reflect a book's content and represent the author's identity. As an author's writing style evolves throughout their career, it is expected that their cover designs will also evolve, as they'll learn which styles appeal to their ideal reader.

Established authors, however, often focus on balancing their need for fresh, eye-catching covers with maintaining a recognizable brand identity. Evolving backlist covers in tandem with genre trends can ensure their core brand remains intact and recognizable to their loyal readers.

So how does an author balance reader expectations with the need for innovation? Start by being transparent. Include your readers in the process, and manage their expectations by sharing upcoming changes. Your cover redesign project can also be used to further connect with your fan base by requesting feedback on social media or in your author newsletter.

Crafting a book cover that entices new readers, honors existing readers, and becomes an integral part of the reader's journey takes research, effort, and commitment. Cover revitalization isn't just a visual transformation; it's a strategic move that can enhance your literary portfolio, reintroduce your titles, and give them the exposure and recognition they deserve. ■

Eryka Parker

### Eryka Parker

Eryka Parker is a book coach, an award-winning developmental editor, and writing instructor. As a women's contemporary author under the pen name Zariah L. Banks, she creates emotional intimacy novels that prove that everyone deserves to feel seen, appreciated, and loved. She lives in Northeast Ohio with her husband and two children and is currently working on her third novel.

# Celebrating Inclusive Stories

## A Q&A WITH DISABILITY BOOK WEEK FOUNDER MARY MECHAM

Author Mary Mecham is passionate enough about books to have a collection of almost three thousand of them in her house. "It's basically a library here," she jokes. She shares the passion with her two daughters, both of whom have rare genetic conditions that carry a range of additional diagnoses, including severe intellectual disability. Mecham reads to them every day—and recently, she decided she wanted to read her daughters a book with a character they could identify with.

First, she scoured her shelves for books with intellectual disability representation. Then she broadened her search to include any books with disabled characters as main characters.

She found sixteen, half of which were from the same series.

The discovery put Mecham on the search for more books with disability representation, especially those written by disabled authors. As her list grew, she wanted to share the stories she'd discovered with others. Three years later, she's doing just that as the founder and current director of Disability Book Week, an annual international event celebrating inclusive literature. The event, which takes place April 23–29, invites the book community to read and promote stories with disability representation, with organizers offering their own recommendations based on the reviews of a sensitivity panel.

*Indie Author Magazine* spoke with Mecham to discuss the importance of inclusive stories and how authors can get involved.

*Note: Responses have been edited for length and clarity.*

## WHY IS DISABILITY REPRESENTATION IMPORTANT IN FICTION?

I don't know if I'm a good person to answer that, because I personally don't have a disability, but on behalf of someone like my daughter, who can't necessarily speak for herself—she's nonverbal—it means so much to be able to identify with a book character. Living with a disability can feel very isolating, so reading a book where there's a character who has the same disability—and then when it's an accurate representation—can help a person feel so seen.

Even if someone doesn't have a disability, I can guarantee they know somebody with a disability. I think the CDC estimated 27 percent of American adults have had a disability at some point in their life or are currently experiencing a disability. That's a fourth of our population. And yet disability-inclusive books are maybe 0.5 percent, 1 percent of books. And that's a huge discrepancy.

## SHOULD NON-DISABLED AUTHORS WRITE DISABILITY-FOCUSED STORIES?

My opinion is that the gold standard is that the individual with the disability writes the book. That is their story. That is what you want, ideally.

Next down is someone who does not have a disability but is very intimately involved in the disability community. An example of this would be a CODA, a child of deaf adults. They grew up in a deaf household. They're very, very familiar with how all that works. They've talked to their parents. They know what that's like, so even though they themselves are not deaf, they are immersed in that world in a way that someone else is not.

And then the next one is an individual who is an author who does not have a disability, but they have an extensive sensitivity panel that screens their book multiple times to make sure that there's no inaccuracies and that the disability is portrayed in a positive and empowering way, that it doesn't go into any of the negative stereotypes that perpetuate myths that are just not true about the disability community.

## WHAT ARE SOME STEREOTYPES THAT AUTHORS SHOULD AVOID?

One of my favorite examples of this is blindness. When we look at popular media, individuals with blindness are usually portrayed as having cloudy eyes and seeing only black. Think of the Jedi in *Star Wars: Rogue One*. He can sense everything around him. Or it's very popular to have an individual who's blind and sees the future—like Mama Odie from *Princess and the Frog*. That's very, very common. And while it's not like we're going to think, "Oh, they can have the Force. They're going to see the future," it is perpetuating that blind people see only black, which is only true for a small percent of individuals with visual impairment.

Another example is autism. Everyone always thinks, "Oh, well, Sheldon Cooper probably has Asperger's, and he's brilliant." So it's things like that, where the intent is good, and they really are trying to be inclusive. They're just not quite sure how to portray that in an accurate manner because they may not have had that experience.

## HOW DO YOU CELEBRATE DISABILITY BOOK WEEK?

Here in the States, we really encourage self-advocates to try and get a proclamation from their mayor, from their governor, which is basically when they write in to their mayor, to their governor, and say, "Hey, we want this recognized in our state or in our town." And then they go around to libraries, to schools, to bookstores, and say, "Hey, could you put up a display? Can you invite an author with a disability?"—just to get it in front of people's eyes and raise that visibility.

We also have our disability board, and they go through and review books—some of them they have just picked up, and some that people will send in to get reviewed. We have a list that can be printed off on our website, and we have a lot of schools and libraries that go onto that website and find all the books or order some to put in their libraries and to put up displays.

## HOW CAN AUTHORS GET INVOLVED?

It's really, really easy to get involved. Just tell your readers, "Hey, guys, I'm participating in a Disability Book Week" or "I'm reading this for Disability Book Week." A lot of authors that we work with that have disability representation in their books will also put their book on sale or things like that, just to try and encourage people to to snag that book, to read it and gain some perspective there.

One of the great things about Disability Book Week is it's so adaptable. We've had people run their book clubs, and then we have schools that have speakers come in. We had librarians—oh, my goodness, they are saints! They are so excited about these things. But they were putting up displays. We have a really strong social media campaign, so for our self-advocates, who are maybe homebound or don't have a lot of mobility, they can still get on their computer and share their message that way. That's what I love about Disability Book Week—there's something for everyone. ■

Nicole Schroeder

### RESOURCES

To see the Disability Book Week's recommended books for disability representation, visit https://disabilitybookweek.org. Submissions are closed for this year's event, but keep an eye on the site for when you can submit your book for consideration in the future.

Rosalie Mastaler's Ultimate Book List compiles disability-inclusive books for all age ranges. Find it at http://rosaliemastaler.com/the-ultimate-book-list.

*Know of any directories or recommended reading lists for finding inclusive titles that we missed? Let us know at feedback@indieauthormagazine.com!*

## Nicole Schroeder

Nicole Schroeder is a storyteller at heart. As the editor in chief of Indie Author Magazine, she brings nearly a decade of journalism and editorial experience to the publication, delighting in any opportunity to tell true stories and help others do the same. She holds a bachelor's degree from the Missouri School of Journalism and minors in English and Spanish. Her previous work includes editorial roles at local publications, and she's helped edit and produce numerous fiction and nonfiction books, including a Holocaust survivor's memoir, alongside independent publishers. Her own creative writing has been published in national literary magazines. When she's not at her writing desk, Nicole is usually in the saddle, cuddling her guinea pigs, or spending time with family. She loves any excuse to talk about Marvel movies and considers National Novel Writing Month its own holiday.

*Your Questions about Book Publicity,*

# ANSWERED

When you write and publish a book, naturally, you want people to read it. The best way to get your book in front of readers is to promote it. "Publicity" is the umbrella term for the steps an author takes to promote their book. Publicity and marketing may include organizing author talks and events, scheduling book reviews and guest articles in newspapers and online, coordinating advertisements, and sending out early copies of the books to readers who will review the book before, during, and after its release date.

Book publicity is a big job. Some authors love it; others find it too time consuming and demanding to handle all aspects of promoting their book on their own. The goal of a professional publicity team is to handle promotion on an author's behalf, so the author can focus on writing their next book while simultaneously getting better promotion than they could coordinate on their own without inside knowledge of literary marketing and public relations strategies.

Below, we're answering some of the biggest questions authors may have about book promotion and the role a publicity company can play.

## WHAT IS THE BIGGEST MISCONCEPTION ABOUT HIRING A MARKETING TEAM FOR YOUR BOOKS?

One of the biggest misconceptions about book marketing and publicity is that a book's story or premise will sell the book on its own.

You really need to think of your book as a product; every aspect of your book should be designed to sell that product. In addition to a great premise, you also need an eye-catching, professionally designed cover, a strong editor, early blurbs and reviews, a solid sales plan that ensures your book is easily accessible in multiple formats—e-book, audio, and the like—and that's just hitting a few basics.

No "one thing" will make a book take off. Many things come together to support a title and give it its best chance at success in the marketplace. Prepare to put the same amount of time and energy into promoting your book as you put into writing it.

## WHAT CAN A MARKETING TEAM DO THAT THE AUTHOR CAN'T?

Someone who specializes in author publicity and book marketing has built up years of experience to ultimately save you time, energy, and headache. Promotional strategies are constantly changing. New opportunities are available each year. Having to sift through all of this information is time consuming at best; at worst, you're actually missing opportunities to maximize your book launch.

A publicist has expertise in elevating your author brand and coordinating effective book marketing. Publicists have also developed relationships with a strong list of book reviewers, social media influencers, booksellers, librarians, and other industry insiders. This means they can efficiently reach the decision-makers who recommend books in media, online, and at bookstores.

Firms like Books Forward work hard to stay ahead of industry trends, tailoring promotional efforts to the author's goals and budget, the book's genre and target audience, and any fresh opportunities that may be available.

In short, publicists make book promotion easier, more efficient, and most effective.

## HOW FAR IN ADVANCE SHOULD AN AUTHOR CONTACT A PUBLICITY FIRM REGARDING THEIR UPCOMING RELEASE?

Reach out to a publicity firm sooner rather than later. Publicists hear from multiple authors each day interested in their services and schedule campaigns many months in advance of the book's launch. A good rule of thumb is to start your publicity about four months prior to the public release date—which means you need to reach out to a firm even sooner to reserve your space in their schedule.

If you're already closer to your book launch, or even post-launch, don't hesitate to reach out and ask for support. While it is good to build a foundation leading up to launch, there are absolutely some worthwhile post-launch promotional tactics to keep momentum going.

## WHAT'S THE BEST WAY FOR AN AUTHOR TO PROMOTE THEIR PREVIOUSLY PUBLISHED BOOKS?

The more books you launch and promote, the better your return will be. You can adver-

tise the first book of a series, the entire series overall, a collection of separate but related titles, or stand-alone titles. There are many advertising opportunities to reach fans of comparable authors directly via social media, retail platforms, book club newsletters and other industry sites.

In addition to targeted advertising, you can breathe new life into a previously released book by

- getting active on social media and joining BookTok challenges;
- connecting your book to something happening in the news cycle, especially if you can provide expert commentary on the issue or trend;
- placing guest articles that intrigue readers and feature links to your books;
- hosting fellow authors at your local bookstore for events where you celebrate the new author's launch while promoting your work at the same time;
- running a promotional price for your e-book that you can advertise;
- honing in further on areas you saw the best traction with your book launch.

There are always more readers to reach!

## WHAT KIND OF TIMELINE SHOULD I CONSIDER FOR PUBLICITY?

You should expect for traditional publicity efforts to begin about four months prior to a book's publication date. Many reviewers and bookish outlets not only expect but require advanced copies of the book to have time to plan their coverage before the general public has access to the title.

Reach out to interview publicity firms even further in advance of that, as many schedule campaigns quite far out.

It is very important to put a strong effort behind your book's launch. This will help build word-of-mouth buzz and spark retailer algorithms. It's also important to note that pre-sales count toward your first week of sales, which can affect whether you hit best-seller lists.

But if you're already post-launch, know that there are plenty of opportunities still available to keep building momentum and readership. It's an outdated way of thinking that books can only be promoted prior to release, and authors shouldn't give up on promotion if they just didn't have the time or resources to devote to the initial launch.

Writing more than one book helps as well. Readers who fall in love with your work will want more, and other new readers will be introduced each time you release a book.

## WHAT WILL MY PUBLICISTS HANDLE? WHAT WILL I BE EXPECTED TO DO?

Book promotion is most effective when authors are involved partners. So yes, even though a professional agency can handle many pieces, you are still the "face" of promotion and will be the one doing the interviews, writing guest articles, networking in person, and so forth. A seasoned publicist should certainly shape the promotional plan to fit your comfort level—perhaps, for example, you love writing guest articles but prefer to not do in-person events. No matter what, you'll have some level of involvement, even if it's simply to review and approve strategies before they are implemented on your behalf.

## LET'S SAY I WRITE THREE DIFFERENT SERIES. SHOULD I EVER PROMOTE THE THREE TOGETHER AS MY BRAND, OR SHOULD I KEEP THEM AS THEIR OWN ENTITIES?

Be strategic with how you promote separate series. If they are within the same genre, you can absolutely promote to the same audiences, but also think about ways each

series is unique and how each may individually appeal to readers. If you are writing across genres, you definitely need to cater to the different target audiences with your promotion.

## IF I PUBLISH UNDER MULTIPLE PEN NAMES, DO I NEED TO CREATE SOCIAL MEDIA PROFILES FOR EACH PEN NAME?

You certainly can, but only do so if you plan to actively run each account. Of course, social media management can be incredibly time consuming, so you may want to focus on a platform you know and understand really well—and actually enjoy—versus running multiple accounts on multiple platforms without giving your all to each of them.

Think about why you chose a pen name. If it was to differentiate from your previous work, you'll need to treat the promotion as such.

## HOW MUCH DOES GOOD BOOK PUBLICITY COST?

Good publicity from a seasoned professional will likely cost more than $5,000, and frankly, you get what you pay for. Publicity is incredibly time-consuming and specialized work.

Some publicity firms, like Books Forward, do offer pro bono services each year, as well as consultations to help set authors on the right path for publicity. Books Forward also offers guided DIY packages and training materials authors can use on their own, so they don't break their budget.

In general, book promotion should be seen as an investment, just like starting any new business. There will be the short-term benefit of immediate exposure to various audiences and the longer-term benefit of accolades and acclaim that support your author brand for years to come as more readers discover your books.

## WHAT SHOULD AUTHORS EXPECT IN TERMS OF SUCCESS?

Think about what success means to you. Does success look like selling lots of books, releasing more than one book, getting a feature in a newspaper, building up your readership, garnering reviews, or something else? Then think about clear, actionable, and realistic steps you can take toward achieving those personalized goals.

If you need some inspiration, check out the case studies on the Books Forward website for various authors with just as varied goals: https://booksforward.com/case-studies.

Most importantly, don't forget to have fun with your promotion. Enjoy the experience as you see readers connect with your work. ∎
Melissa DeCuir

### Melissa DeCuir

A former award-winning journalist, Marissa DeCuir now helps authors share their stories and messages with the world as president of Books Forward publicity and Books Fluent publishing. The companies are committed to elevating voices and breaking barriers in book promotion. Interested in what's possible for your book sales and building readership? Check out our services, tell us your goals and get a customized publicity campaign tailored just for you: booksforward.com

# An Author's Notes on Notion, the Customizable Productivity Platform

The author's technology stack—that is, the digital tool set they use to conduct business—is ever-changing. Technology grows and develops, adding features and functionality, solutions to problems that may not have arisen yet. Notion aims to fit into this category, offering an all-in-one organization and productivity tool for individuals and teams. It is a database, a kanban board, a grocery list, and more, and depending on your individual needs, it may have a place in your author workflow.

Notion offers both free and paid tiers for individual users, as well as two upper-level tiers for larger companies. Notion Plus, designed for individual users and small groups, costs $8 per user per month, billed annually, or $10 per user per month, billed monthly; however, most of the platform's features are available at the same functionality for those with the free version of Notion. Read on to learn about the program and how it could come in handy for organizing your author business.

## CUSTOMIZABLE WORKSPACES

Notion offers a variety of tools designed to be easy to use and robust from the outset, allowing the platform to become a space for project management, note-taking, database management, wikis, or more. Users can decide on sharing and permission settings to allow collaborators on specific dashboards, so authors have the flexibility to bring on a virtual assistant to work on a specific project or invite cover designers to a teamspace. Most impressive is Notion's ability to take on databases, synced calendars, and thirty-plus projects at once and keep it organized throughout the application. Notion allows you to customize fonts, layout, structure, and shareability, removing accessibility issues and information bottlenecks.

## INTEGRATED NOTE-TAKING

Plenty of authors search for sticky notes, notebooks, or a spare napkin when struck by inspiration. Notion can serve as a replacement for your serviette with its features designed for quick and organized note-taking, allowing users to write, plan, and organize their thoughts and projects seamlessly. Within the app, you can format your notes with headings, texts, fonts, highlights, images, and even emoji icons using keyboard shortcuts in the program or by highlighting the text and hovering over the format menu that appears. Users familiar with Microsoft Word or OneNote should feel at home.

**Pro Tip:** You can keep notes private, share them with your team, or make them public, as well as enable collaborative editing and in-line comments. This is perfect for team members to collaborate on thoughts and ideas.

## DATABASE FUNCTIONALITY

Notion's functionality as a database is comparable to Excel or Numbers. Databases are a collection of pages within Notion; each item within the database is an editable page with customizable properties such as links, labels, and dates, so you can add additional details and notes as needed to an entry.

Notion allows users to transform databases using a multitude of layouts pre-built into the application to help you visualize your information. This means you can view your database as a board, list, calendar, gallery, or timeline without having to reformat the information by hand.

**Pro Tip:** Consider using a database to track keywords, categories, or other metadata for books or series.

## TASK AND PROJECT MANAGEMENT

An author's publishing process has plenty of steps involved, including planning, drafting, and marketing, and authors often have a particular strategy for managing their books. Notion facilitates task management with features such as to-do lists, kanban boards, and reminders, allowing for both functionality and customization for the individual author's needs. Additionally, users can assign deadlines, subtasks, or progress tags to a project to provide context to a task or further organize their to-do lists. Notion centralizes the work you or your team conducts, allowing for advanced automations and workflows.

## COLLABORATION TOOLS

With Notion's built-in collaboration tools, users can add members, administrators, guests, and groups to a dashboard, as well as control collaborators' access to specific pages within a dashboard as needed. The free version of the program allows for up to ten guests, but paying users can invite one hundred to two hundred fifty guests, depending on their tier.

**Pro Tip:** Use Notion's Updates and Notifications to stay on top of tasks and assignments that need attention. Similar to Facebook's tagging feature, you can receive notifications in real time whenever someone @mentions you or replies to a comment.

## TEMPLATE OPTIONS

Notion tries to take the guesswork out of project management by providing templates for many use cases, from personal productivity trackers to business management. Templates are also shareable, meaning other users of the platform can create custom templates and publish them online. Some of these templates may be free, and some are paid, but Notion's website has over one thousand templates available at no cost at https://notion.so/templates. Notion also pays creators who apply for their template creation program to add value to their database and ever-growing template list.

## INTEGRATION CAPABILITIES

Notion can integrate with more than eighty other platforms to collect and centralize data, files, and other information. These platforms range from other productivity aids, like Trello, to collaboration apps, such as Slack; file storage platforms, like Dropbox, Box, or Google Drive; and automation software, like Zapier. Notion acts as a live data stream for external tools, syncing them in real time.

Like templates, integrations are also listed on Notion's website, available for immediate connection. View the platform's current available integrations at https://notion.so/integrations/all.

**Pro Tip:** Notion also has its own AI tool, available for unlimited use at paid tiers, that can answer questions, autofill responses, and help brainstorm written content.

## DOCUMENT AND CONTENT STORAGE

Users can store documents and other content within Notion, making it a true database of information rather than a table of contents. If stored locally, drag files into a Notion page from your desktop or folder on your computer. Files can also be imported from outside apps, like Dropbox or Google Drive.

Some documents, such as PDFs, can be embedded and provide a preview directly in the program. Others can be stored in Notion and downloaded onto other devices. Notion accepts most document types, including video, as long as the streaming service has embedded links enabled.

## CROSS-PLATFORM COMPATIBILITY

Authors are always on the go, and whether you primarily conduct business on your laptop, phone, or desktop, Notion is able to sync across devices through its native cross-platform application. It is cloud-based software, so users can access their dashboard through the app or any browser window.

**Pro Tip:** Some features in Notion are available offline, but functionality is not guaranteed given that it's cloud-based software. If you need to access Notion without a Wi-Fi connection, try leaving the page open in a browser and making changes as needed while offline. The page will then update when you reconnect to the internet.

## CUSTOMIZABLE ACCESS AND PERMISSIONS

Along with its collaborative environments, Notion allows users to set specific access levels and permissions for different team members or external collaborators, with options such as "View Only" or "Editor." Full-access administrators have top-level permissions, including the ability to add and remove team members and change workspace settings, but the "Can edit content" role will suffice for most other team members.

## ALL-IN-ONE TOOL

Author needs considered, Notion is a robust, customizable powerhouse in terms of functionality, and, with a range of free and paid tiers, it can be a useful piece of software capable of streamlining most tasks. However, there is the argument that authors may not need all the functionality of the system or feel the desire to learn the technology to utilize it to its fullest potential. The lack of complete offline use may also be prohibitive to authors who often find themselves away from a stable internet connection.

As always, consider your needs and make the best decisions for your business, and if in doubt, give the system a test run with the Free plan to decide if it will fit into your technology stack. For the author who wants an all-in-one organizational platform with complete customization and the ability to collaborate, Notion may be worth a try. ■

David Viergutz

### David Viergutz

David Viergutz is a disabled Army Veteran, Law Enforcement Veteran, husband and proud father. He is an author of stories from every flavor of horror and dark fiction. One day, David's wife sat him down and gave him the confidence to start putting his imagination on paper. From then on out his creativity has no longer been stifled by self-doubt and he continues to write with a smile on his face in a dark, candle-lit room.

# From the Stacks

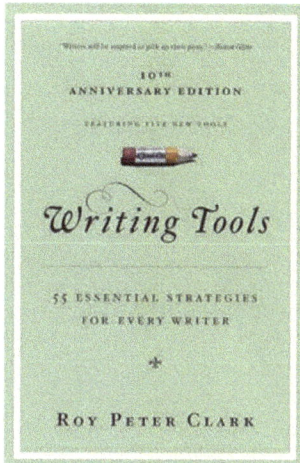

**Book:** *Writing Tools: 55 Essential Strategies for Every Writer*
https://www.indieauthortools.com/books/writing-tools-55-essential-strategies-for-every-writer

A collection of thirty years of wisdom, *Writing Tools: 55 Essential Strategies for Every Writer* by Roy Peter Clark is a series of essays on the different aspects of writing. The book provides over two hundred examples from journalism and literature and fifty essays by Clark himself, all divided into an easy-to-digest format of four separate sections: Special Effects, Blueprints for Stories, Useful Habits, and Nuts and Bolts. Noted as a classic guidebook for novice and expert writers alike, the tenth-anniversary version of the book now includes five brand new tools.

**Tool: Font Squirrel Matcherator**
https://www.indieauthortools.com/website-tools-apps/font-squirrel-matcherator

Having matching fonts across your social media channels, your covers, or even your newsletters provides credibility and a uniform brand identity. Font Squirrel Matcherator takes the guesswork out of discovering what font was used, allowing you to search for fonts used by uploading a picture. This is perfect if you can't remember what font you used or if you want to identify another creator's font.

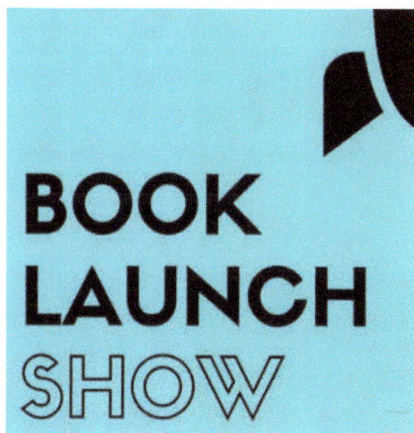

**Podcast:** *Book Launch Show*
https://podcasts.apple.com/gb/podcast/book-launch-show/id1185641344

Tim Grahl is a marketing consultant, CEO, and publisher at Story Grid. Grahl boasts helping launch multiple books into the *New York Times*, *Wall Street Journal*, and other bestseller lists and moonlights as the host of the *Book Launch Show* podcast. He says the episodes are short, to the point, and packed with tactics that are still widely relevant today. Grahl focuses on the fundamentals of selling books and provides information in an easy-to-understand, step-by-step method.

# When Fantasy Invades Reality

## EXPLORING THE FANTASTIC IN THE MUNDANE WITH THE MAGICAL REALISM GENRE

An old man with giant, feathered wings is discovered lying face-down on the ground, and the whole town comes out to see him—until a carnival arrives, and they lose interest.

For a moment, Gabriel Garcia Marquez's short story "A Very Old Man With Enormous Wings" sounds like the start of a typical Fantasy, but the story blends something extraordinary with gritty depictions of the natural world and treats a clearly supernatural being as a mere curiosity—a contradiction typical of Magical Realism. The genre emphasizes the mundane aspects of marvelous creatures and elements to such a degree that when magical things happen, characters accept them as a part of everyday life. By blurring the lines between Realistic Fiction and Fantasy, authors draw attention to the absurdity and mysteries of reality.

Although it is often confused with subgenres of Fantasy, due to the magical elements at play, Magical Realism is more directly linked to Realist and Speculative Fiction. Traditionally, stories that fall under Fantasy categories are characterized by their creation of a new reality. Even Urban Fantasies, which take place in modern settings, build worlds that play by different rules than ours and usually follow those rules consistently. In Magical Realism, the author makes no attempt to explain the fantastic elements and the uncanny chaos that occurs when they appear in an otherwise mundane setting. Readers are meant to feel unsettled by the contrast.

## HISTORY

Compared with other fantastical genres, Magical Realism is fairly new to the literary world. German art critic Franz Roh coined the term "magic realism" in 1925 to describe a style of painting that was also viewed as "fantastical," "marvelous," and "surreal." The artists pushed the boundaries of Realism by portraying fantastical elements as part of the rational world. Their works influenced many writers of the time, including Italian writer Massimo Bontempelli, who founded a magic realist magazine in 1926.

In 1955, a literary critic first used the term "magical realism" in his essay on the works of Argentine author Jorge Luis Borges. Magical Realism continues to be best associated with the work of Latin American authors, like Isabel Allende and Laura

Esquivel. However, writers from many cultures have contributed to the genre, including Toni Morrison, Haruki Murakami, Salman Rushdie, Yann Martel, and Neil Gaiman.

## CONTROVERSY

In a 2014 article for *Vox*, Kelsey McKinney details some of the debates around the genre, primarily concerns about cultural appropriation. "Because magical realism was popularized in countries that had been colonized, scholars like Brahim Barhoun of the University of Madrid see the adoption of magical realism into mainstream literature by commercial writers as cultural appropriation," writes McKinney. The use of Magical Realism to make social commentary, particularly anti-imperialist sentiments, ties the literature to political movements, including Latin American nationalism.

Others argue that while Magical Realism was popularized in Latin America, the genre has Western roots and global applications. Angel Flores, author of *Magical Realism in Spanish America*, says that "Magical realism is a continuation of the romantic realist tradition of Spanish language literature and its European counterparts," and as such should not be considered exclusive to Latin America, though it should be recognized as having a "Hispanic birthplace." Indeed, McKinney says that "a case could be made that magical realism and the Latin American 'Boom' also paved the way for later literary movements by underrepresented groups like the postcolonial literature" of authors like Margaret Atwood and Naguib Mahfouz.

## MAGIC IN MODERN LIFE

Although Magical Realism continues to be popular among readers who also enjoy Speculative Fiction, Fairytale Retellings, Cozy Fantasy, and Urban Fantasy, there are still people who might not recognize the term, particularly outside of a Latin American social context. This can make it difficult to market since some of your potentially most-dedicated readers won't think to search this category. Because of this, you'll often find Magical Realism books shelved under the next-closest genre. *The Water Dancer* by Ta-Nehisi Coates, for example, sometimes appears under Historical Fiction or Science Fiction. Zoraida Cordova's *The Inheritance of Orquídea Divina* is often

labeled Paranormal or Urban Fantasy. Several of Adrienne Young's and Sarah Addison Allen's books are tagged as Women's Fiction, despite being driven by elements of Magical Realism.

In general, Magical Realism tends to be viewed as a more literary approach to magic than any of the subgenres of Fantasy. It seems to be most successful when it's published as an upmarket work.

## CHARACTERISTICS OF MAGICAL REALISM

- **Realistic Setting:** Usually contemporary; a modern time and place
- **Magical or Fantastical elements**, which are accepted as normal by the characters
- **Limited Information (Authorial Reticence):** No explanation is given for the existence of magical or fantastical elements
- **Political or Social Critique:** Often told from a marginalized perspective, these stories offer criticism of those in power.

## RESOURCES

PBS: *Why Magical Realism is a Global Phenomenon* | It's Lit (https://www.youtube.com/watch?v=scgn2BCcht4)

"What Is Magical Realism? Definition and Examples of Magical Realism in Literature, Plus 7 Magical Realism Novels You Should Read" by Masterclass: https://www.masterclass.com/articles/what-is-magical-realism

"11 Questions You're Too Embarrassed To Ask About Magical Realism" by Kelsey McKinney, *Vox*: https://www.vox.com/2014/4/20/5628812/11-questions-youre-too-embarrassed-to-ask-about-magical-realism

"For The Last Time: What Is The Difference Between Fantasy And Magical Realism?" by AJ Vrana (https://thechaoscycle.com/what-is-the-difference-between-fantasy-and-magical-realism/)

"10 Must-Read Magical Realism Books for a Touch of Enchantment" by Robyn Moreno, *Reader's Digest*: https://www.rd.com/list/magical-realism-books/ ■

Jenn Lessmann

### Jenn Lessmann

Jenn Lessmann is the author of Unmagical: a Witchy Mystery and three stories on Kindle Vella. A former barista, stage manager, and high school English teacher with advanced degrees from impressive colleges, she continues to drink excessive amounts of caffeine, stay up later than is absolutely necessary, and read three or four books at a time. Jenn is currently studying witchcraft and the craft of writing, and giggling internally whenever they intersect. She writes snarky paranormal fantasy for new adults whenever her dog will allow it.

# Writing in Abundance

If you've been reading this column for a while and focusing on shifting your money mindset, you might have experienced a shift in your productivity too.

Perhaps you are now thinking, "How can I take it to the next level?" More specifically, "How can I get into some serious writing abundance?"

As an author, you want more words … because more words equals more books, right? More books means growth for your author business and a chance to see that shift in your money mindset pay dividends. The good news here—and it's all good news—is that stepping into the flow of abundance can be fast and easy.

It may take time, but in just three steps, you can train yourself to write with abundance.

**Step One: Choose your word count.** You need more words, but how many more do you need? Pick a word count you can, almost without effort, write every single day. Hint: make it easy to succeed and hard to fail. Stephen King writes 2,500 words every day, so that's easy for him. For me, when I'm writing a book, I strive for one thousand words a day. That's after almost twenty years; if I were starting now, I'd focus on writing one hundred words—yep, just one hundred. It shouldn't be an astounding number; pick a goal you know you can hit, no matter what.

**Step Two: Start your streak.** Set a goal to write your words every single day for thirty days. One day will become two, seven will become twenty, and twenty will become thirty. Print out a calendar and mark off the days you've completed your writing, or use an app like Habit Tracker. The bonus benefit of using an app is you can set a reminder for later in the day, just in case you get off-track. More than once, I've kept one of my streaks in the very last moments before my head hit the pillow.

**Step Three: Schedule your writing.** An intention without an appointment is like a wish without a plan. My daily writing hour begins at 5:30 a.m. The coffeepot and teapot are set up the night before, my work-in-progress is the only document open on my computer, and my alarm sounds at 5:25 a.m. that it's time for refills and words. What gets measured gets done, as does what is scheduled. Make your writing the priority you say that it is, and the words will indeed flow in abundance.

Of course, life happens. If you miss one day, just don't miss two. If you miss two days, press the reset button, and for the love of book launches, don't miss three! Remember why you wanted to do all of this writing in the first place. Take a deep breath, put your shoulders back, and write.

## THE BENEFITS

There are tons of benefits to setting a word count goal, having a streak, and checking off those thirty days of writing. But allow me to share one very important benefit: you will feel absolutely incredible. You will have proven to yourself, beyond any doubt, that you can write an abundance of words—because you will have done it. The self-confidence that will follow this accomplishment will astound you.

With some focus and dedication, an abundance of words will flow from your fingertips, and when they do, I hope you'll write and tell me all about it. ■

Honorée Corder

## Honorée Corder

Honorée Corder is the author of more than fifty books, an empire builder, and encourager of writers. When she's not writing, she's spoiling her dog and two cats, eating something fabulous her husband made on the grill, working out, or reading. She hopes this article made a positive impact on your life, and if it did, you'll reach out to her via HonoreeCorder. com.

# Habits, the Atomic Way

## THREE LESSONS JAMES CLEAR'S 'ATOMIC HABITS' OFFERS AUTHORS FOR REACHING THEIR WRITING GOALS

Since it was published in 2018, James Clear's book, *Atomic Habits*, has sold over fifty million copies and been translated into fifty languages. The book offers tips for any adult looking to improve their lives with better habits, but for authors and self-employed creatives especially, Clear's concepts offer a chance to build better, more sustainable business strategies through regular practice.

"Every action you take is a vote for the type of person you wish to become," Clear writes. Authors are aiming for a satisfying, sustainable, and reliable career. Regardless of the presence of financial specifics, goals set the direction. But to get moving in that direction, we need systems and processes that support those goals. Clear's book shares more in-depth concepts to smooth the way through those uncomfortable changes, but here are three key lessons we can use.

**Lesson 1: Use good habits to your advantage** to improve by a small margin—even 1 percent—per day. Over time, those small gains snowball into successes and habits that put goals within your reach. For example, if you haven't been writing at all, scheduling time to write is a step toward your goal. Making it into a habit by sitting down to write with your first cup of coffee will get you another step toward building the habit. This temptation bundling—rewarding the habit you need to form with the one tied to something you want—will cue your brain to do the habit you are trying to form and improve the chances of success.

**Lesson 2: Focus on systems instead of goals**. Without realizing it, you may have fallen into habits that don't support your goals. Time to pivot! It's definitely not easy, but in the example of struggling with writing, you need to build in a system that helps you write. Block out time, and be sure you have the tech, childcare, environment, and space needed to get work done effectively.

*Lesson One*

*Lesson Two*

lesson
Three

**Lesson 3: Create your identity and build supportive habits around it.** Call yourself a writer, then prove it to yourself over and over again. All it takes is a small win. So when you sit and write, take a moment to think of yourself as a writer. Writers write, so the more often you do this, the more you'll reinforce the habit of writing—and around the cycle goes. ▪

Jen B. Green

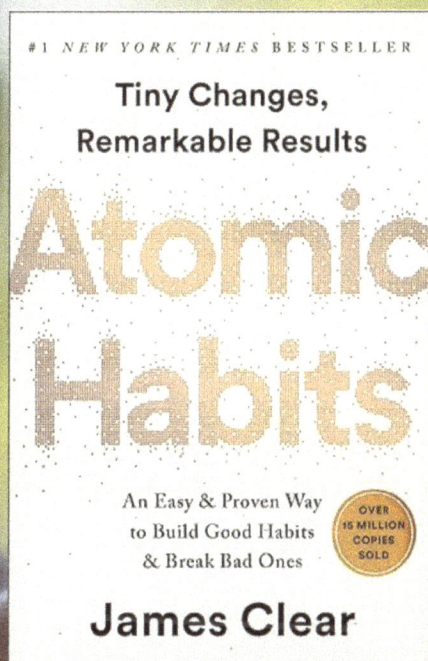

#1 *NEW YORK TIMES* BESTSELLER

Tiny Changes,
Remarkable Results

Atomic
Habits

An Easy & Proven Way
to Build Good Habits
& Break Bad Ones

OVER
15 MILLION
COPIES
SOLD

**James Clear**

## Jen B. Green

Jen B. Green has lived in five countries on four continents with her three sons, two daughters, and one great guy. She reads anything that stays still long enough, plays piano, and bakes everything sweet.

After earning her Ph.D. in psychology, Jen tried writing a novel for Nanowrimo and was hooked! Her days are spent traveling the world, teaching undergraduate psychology, and wrangling her growing homemade army, but her nights are for writing Urban Fantasy with witches and werewolves.

# CORNER THE MARKET

# What's the Deal with BookBub Featured Deals?

The ever-elusive BookBub Featured Deal: with all the work some authors will put in to land one, it's easy for anyone new to the tool to wonder if they're truly worth the hype. But whether you have never applied for a BookBub Featured Deal or applied, didn't get one, and have long since given up, I implore you to submit your titles.

BookBub is not the only paid promotion platform out there, but some will argue that it is currently the best, or at least that its promotions have the greatest impact on an author's sales.

So what is it?

BookBub is a subscription service, much like your newsletter. The people they email are interested enough in books to get an email from BookBub every day telling them what bargains are available.

"Bargains" is a key word. You do not have to lower your book price to $0.99 or make it free for a Featured Deal, but it pays to keep in mind that you will compete with other titles both to secure a promotion spot and to get the subscribers' attention when the email goes out.

Here's how you can apply for a spot in that email.

On BookBub's author dashboard, the Featured Deal button can be found in the left-side column beneath My Promotions. That will take you to the Featured Deals page, where you can apply to have BookBub promote your book to their subscribers.

You can offer a single title—first-in-series is an obvious choice, though it can be your latest in the series or any other book you might wish to push—or you can offer a boxed set. In the past, I have had the most success promoting boxed sets.

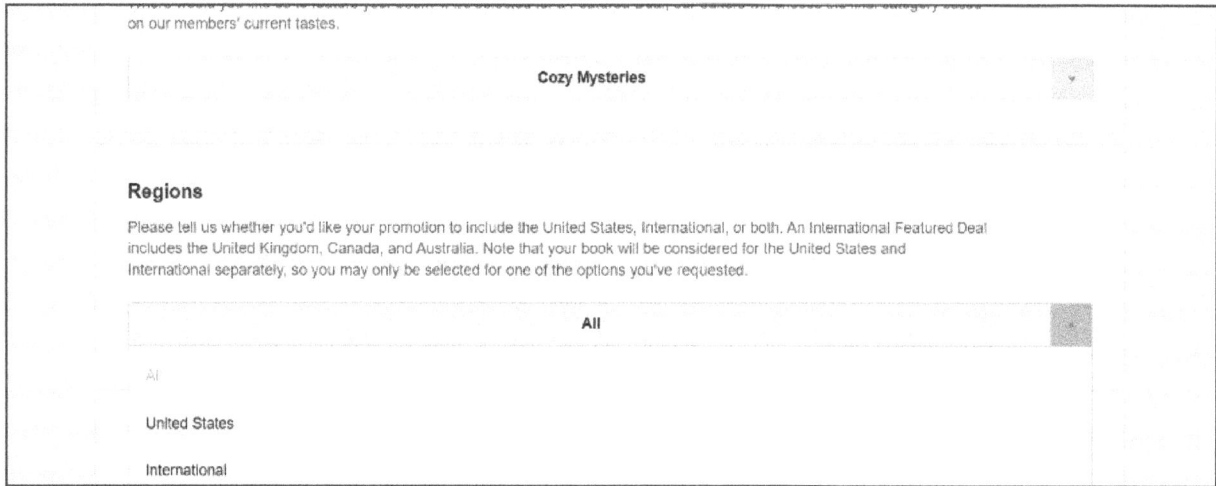

Once you've decided which title or boxed set to promote, you must select the genre for your book and where you want it to be promoted. Here, select the option for all regions. The US deal is significantly more expensive than the international deal, but its effectiveness is significantly greater.

## COST

BookBub Featured Deals are expensive. "Expensive" isn't necessarily a recognized unit of measurement, but a Cozy Mystery deal for all regions costs more than $1,000 for a one-day promotion.

However, if you set it up correctly, it can be worth it.

Look not at what you spend but at how much money you make in return. When I promoted ten Cozy Mystery books, I dropped the price to $0.99 using the 35 percent royalty option, not a Kindle Countdown Deal (KCD). The promotion cost a shade over $1,000 but made that money back within a couple of hours of the promotion going live. It propelled the title to number four in the Amazon.com chart, and as a result, it stayed in the top two hundred or three hundred titles for the next ninety days, racking up more than twenty thousand page-reads per day and netting about $30,000 more than it otherwise would have with my normal advertising.

So why not use a KCD? Following the promotion, I wanted to keep the price low, and a KCD would have automatically returned to full price at the end of the countdown period. Instead, I reset the price to $5.99 the day after the promotion ended and took advantage of its high chart position and visibility. Only when sales began to die off did I return the title to full price.

## WIDE OR AMAZON-EXCLUSIVE?

Being available only on Amazon may impact your chances of getting a Featured Deal. However, this is anecdotal evidence, not empirical; you can assume that this is accurate, but apply anyway. I have never been wide but have enjoyed many BookBub Featured Deals.

I just keep applying.

Of course, BookBub isn't the only option. There are deal-of-the-day features on several platforms, and most of them have proven worth the investment. Whatever you do, believe that you need exposure to readers' eyes if you want to sell books. That will almost always cost money, but it can absolutely be worth it to your author career. ■

Steve Higgs

### Steve Higgs

High school Valedictorian enlists in the Marine Corps under a guaranteed tank contract. An inauspicious start that was quickly superseded by excelling in language study.